Simply Science

AGE OF TECHNOLOGY

Gerry Bailey

Illustrations: Steve Boulter & Q2A Media

AUTHOR: **GERRY BAILEY**
CONSULTANT: **STEVE WAY**
EDITOR: **FELICIA LAW**
ILLUSTRATORS:
               STEVE BOULTER
               Q2A MEDIA
DESIGN: **RALPH PITCHFORD**

PHOTO CREDITS:

p.5 WizData, Inc./Shutterstock Inc.
p.15 David C. Baker/Shutterstock Inc.
p.16 Phanie/Rex Features.
p.17 Lester Lefkowitz/CORBIS.
p.19 Marek Slusarczyk/Shutterstock Inc.
p.21 (t) PA/Topfoto, (b) Phillipe Plailly/
SCIENCE PHOTO LIBRARY.
p.25 Andrew Barker/Shutterstock Inc.
p.28 Brian Bell / SCIENCE PHOTO LIBRARY.
p.29 (t) Transport Stock/Rex features,
(b) Dean Conger/CORBIS.

Cover
Zhiltsov Alexandr/Shutterstock Inc.

ISBN 978-1-906292-10-2
Printed in China

AGE OF TECHNOLOGY

Contents

What is technology?

Can you imagine a world with no mobile phones, televisions or even CD players? Probably not. But just a few years ago these things didn't exist. They're all the result of lots of science discoveries and inventions that have been made very recently. The science that helped make these, and many more inventions, is called technology.

We use technology to ...

... listen to the latest hits

... find information on the Web

... watch a favourite film

... heat a whole mealin seconds

... talk to people in countries far away.

Technology in our home

Look around you. There are probably lots of gadgets in your home that you use every day without thinking about them. But they're all products of technology – even the kitchen toaster!

plasma television

toaster

digital radio/ MP3 player

digital camcorder

microwave oven

washing machine

iron

radio controlled car

Let's find out about these kinds of technology:

computers
digital signals
microprocessors
mobile phones
the Internet

...and lots more

The fax

The facsimile machine, or fax for short, sends a written message or picture through the telephone system.

Inside a fax machine is a device that is 'light sensitive'. This means it can tell how much light is coming off the surface of a piece of paper.

If there is an image on the paper, the device will see all the light and dark areas on it. The different amounts of light are then changed to an electronic code that can be sent to another fax.

This receiving fax decodes the message and prints the light and dark areas on another sheet of paper.

1. At first, all letters and pictures and other information had to be sent by mail. It could take ages for a letter to arrive.

2. One inventor made a machine that could transmit a letter by telegraph. But it didn't work very well. A carrier pigeon would have worked better!

3. If words and pictures could be changed into a code of electric pulses, then it might be possible. But an ordinary copying machine couldn't do that!

4. Scientists decided it could be possible to change words into some kind of electronic code.

5. It would then speed things up if the electronic messages could be sent down the telephone. What was needed was a combined copy machine and telephone network.

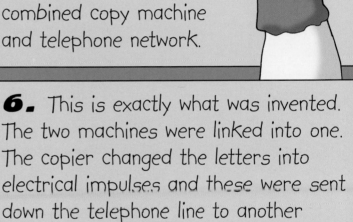

6. This is exactly what was invented. The two machines were linked into one. The copier changed the letters into electrical impulses and these were sent down the telephone line to another machine at the other end.

Digits

Who'd have thought our modern technology could be run on just two numbers, 0 and 1. That's all it takes to program the most complicated computer, or send the best sound or picture to your television set.

Two digits

When we count, we use the decimal system. Decimal means counting in tens, and we use ten digits, zero to nine. But computers count using a different system – BINARY. Zero and one make up what we call the binary system. Binary means two of something and there are just two digits, 0 and 1 in this digital system.

Codes

You can't send your actual voice over the phone or a real picture over a computer. But you can translate the sounds of your voice or the colours in the picture into a special code. The code can be made into a series of electric pulses that travel along wires, or made into sound waves that travel from one antenna to another.

A code that copied

The first technology machines used a code system called analogue. Analogue means 'similar to'. So the sounds or electric pulses were 'similar to' a voice or to the the light and dark parts of a picture.

Digital technology

Today's high tech machines use the digital system of 0 and 1. This means your voice or a picture are translated into a digital code of 0's and 1's. Your name, for example, would end up as a row of 0's and 1's. A 1 digit would become an electric pulse or maybe a sound wave, while a zero would be a blank space.

The computer

A computer is an electronic machine that can record and recall information very quickly.

A task, or job, is put into the computer, usually using a keyboard. A screen, or monitor, shows the information. This is then stored in the computer's memory.

If we linked our brains, we might be able to invent a smaller computer.

An electronic brain

1. The first computers built in the early 1900s took up a lot of space. They were filled with vacuum tubes and other large pieces of equipment. These computers were also very expensive. Only governments and big companies could afford to use them.

2. Things changed in 1947 when the transistor was invented. But computers were still too big to put on top of a desk.

A *personal computer*

Today a personal computer, or PC, can be used by everyone and can fit easily onto a desktop. Inside the computer is a tiny microprocessor that operates it. Personal computers use different programmes to do different tasks. The most popular programmes are word processing programmes that help produce all kinds of documents – like this book!

3. They were certainly too big for people to have at home.

4. Then, in the 1958, the silicone chip was invented. This tiny computer, or microprocessor, could carry a whole circuit, crammed into a tiny space. A computer could run on just a handful of these chips. Now, at last, a small computer could be built.

5. In 1977, Steven Jobs and Stephen Wozniak built an inexpensive personal computer. It was the Apple II and one of the most important inventions in the world.

The microprocessor

A microprocessor is a kind of computer chip. It's the tiny part of the machine that carries out all the instructions in a computer program.

You can find microprocessors in lots of different devices. They are in digital watches, computer games and even in microwave ovens.

Some devices, including large computers, contain more than one microprocessor.

A microprocessor only goes wrong when an error known as a 'bug' or virus gets into a program.

Chips at work

1. The first microprocessors were made to be used in missiles and satellites and not for everyday gadgets like washing machines. But soon, manufacturers of household machines wanted to use them too, to improve the way their products worked.

2. Microprocessors also saved money. For example, computerised robots were much cheaper and more reliable at doing some jobs than humans.

3. In time, large computers were replaced by small ones – controlled by microprocessors.

4. In fact, the microprocessor is the brain of a computer. It is quick, reliable and can store a huge amount of information.

5. Today microprocessors are even more powerful, storing valuable information, or data, on computers. They are essential for running businesses.

High-tech health

Technology helps us in many ways. It's helped to produce wonderful machinery that hospitals use to keep us healthy, including one that can read our brains and another that tracks our heartbeats.

CAT scanner

CAT scanner stands for Computerised Axial Tomographic Scanner – and, despite its name, it's not used to scan furry pussycats! It's used for taking pictures of the inside of the body, including the brain. It uses lots of very thin X-ray beams and detectors to get this information, and then feeds it into a computer. A CAT scan can tell you if your brain is injured or sick in any way.

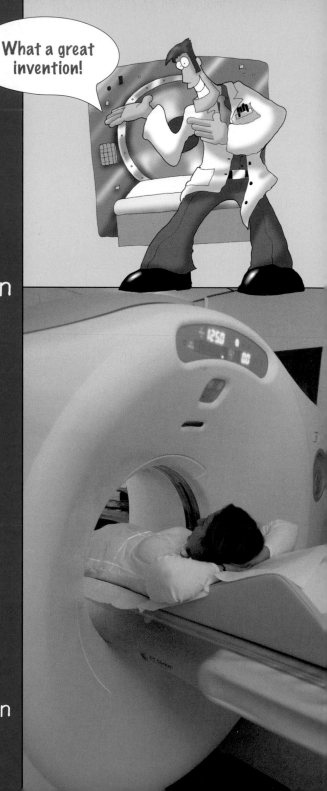

What a great invention!

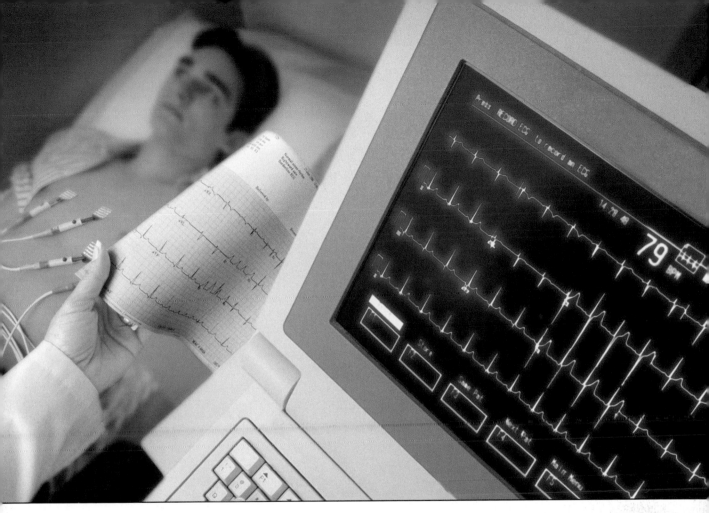

Electro-cardiograph

This machine records what is happening in your heart. Tiny electrical impulses, or currents, pass through your heart each time it beats. The doctors measure a normal pattern of these impulses, then they can tell whenever something is not normal. The electrocardiograph machine records the impulses and prints them out as lines on a graph known as an electro-cardiogram, or ECG.

17

The cell phone

A cellular, or cell, phone, is a telephone that transmits messages using radio signals instead of wires. The signals are transmitted from large antennas that are placed around the countryside.

Talking with no wires

1. Not so very long ago, all telephones were connected to wires. This meant, for example, they were difficult to use on the beach!

2. The first overhead telephone wires were thick and really spoiled the view. Luckily, special wires were invented that could take many signals at once. Now, not so many wires were needed.

The network

Cell phone callers use a special network to make calls. A network has a central exchange in each cell. Calls are collected at the cell, then transmitted to other cells via an open-air transmitter.

3. However, even inventions like automatic telephone exchanges and telephones with push buttons, didn't make any difference – the phones still needed wires!

4. Then scientists started to use radio waves and not wires to carry telephone messages. Now portable phones were possible, although they had to stay close to the power source to keep the signal.

5. Then came satellite technology! Now there were huge aerials everywhere known as antennas. Each gave out a signal over a small area, or cell. So when a caller moved out of one cell, their call would automatically be taken over by the next one.

The CD

A CD, or compact disc, is a round, hard piece of flat plastic coated with a soft metal called aluminium.

CDs are mostly used to store music. They can store up to 80 minutes of sound. This is carried in a spiral around the disc. But instead of the grooves that old records used to have, CDs use a series of hollows called pits. The flat surfaces in between are called flats.

The spiral of flats and pits is read by a laser beam in a special CD player. The player turns the light into electric signals to produce the sound.

1. The first record players, or phonographs, made it possible for people to listen to music for the first time in their own homes. The sound quality wasn't very good as the sound was recorded on a cylinder.

From light to sound

2. Next came the flat disc and gramophone. The first discs were made out of a resin called shellac which is made by insects.

3. Luckily for the insects, the shellac discs were soon replaced by vinyl ones. Vinyl is a kind of tough plastic. The sound was stored in wiggly grooves cut around the disc.

4. There was still some background noise. To solve the problem, inventors started to look at laser technology. Laser is a form of light. A beam of laser light would act as a needle. Dents in the disc would take the place of grooves.

5. Each time the laser light beam hits a dent, or pit as it is known, different electrical signals are sent out. These are changed into different sounds which is what we hear.

New horizons

Technology has allowed us to explore new horizons, such as space and the world of the oceans. Super computers have powered astronauts to the Moon, while miniature submarines can now explore wrecks and wildlife far below the surface of the sea.

Submersibles

Many submersibles today are operated by remote control. Technology involving computers and digital cameras, means divers don't have to swim in places that are too dangerous or too deep.

Virtual reality

A really new place can be anywhere you want to go. Not possible? It is with virtual reality. A computer creates a whole world for you. You can fight dragons or visit the centre of the Earth!

Radio telescope

A radio telescope collects radio signals from space. The radio waves are turned into electrical signals and their strength and the way they travel is recorded.

A computer can then tell where they came from and what caused them in the first place.

Spectrograph

A spectrograph analyses light that comes from stars in space. It breaks this light into the colours of the spectrum. The arrangement of the colours can tell what any star is made of.

Network to the world

1. In the 1960s, the US Army wanted to develop a communications system that would survive a major enemy attack.

2. This got the scientists excited. They began to work on a way to make a network of computers 'talk' to each other.

They developed a system known as ARPAnet. It allowed the computer systems of four universities in the USA to communicate with each other.

3. Of course, everyone wanted to join in – to create a SUPER-network!

4. The idea of one giant network that linked all the small networks in the world was really exciting. This soon happened, and the new, huge supernetwork was called the Internet.

5. Then a computer expert called Tim Berners-Lee wrote a software program that allowed sound, pictures and images to be sent all over the world on the Internet.

The Web

The Web, or World Wide Web, is part of a computer network known as the Internet. It is made up of electronic addresses called websites.

The web works like a giant encyclopaedia. It provides text, sound, pictures and moving images that bring information to every Web user. The Web can also be used to create design, audio and video projects.

Into the future

We already see some amazing technology around us. But what will we be using in the future? Some gadgets give a hint at how things might be.

Universal communicator

Future mobile phones will be able to translate calls into any foreign language. Looking further ahead, radio or light technology might allow us to use phones to talk with aliens – if there are any!

HMD

An HMD is a head mounted display. It's like a computer screen that you wear. Today, HMDs are used by pilots to help fly military aircraft. They are also used to create virtual reality environments for games. But perhaps one day we'll wear one to watch a show instead of watching on an old-fashioned television screen.

Flying car

Flying cars will have room for two people. You'll take off from a field near your home and fly where you like. After landing, you'll detach the fixed wing from your vehicle and continue by road – just as if you were travelling by car.

Jet pack

A jet pack stuntman flew at the opening of the 1984 Los Angeles Olympics. But fuel packs are still heavy and you can't travel far, so who knows...

Force fields

In science fiction, a force field or protective shield is a barrier made up of energy to protect a person from attack.

Boffins have now invented an electric 'force field' that protects armoured vehicles against anti-tank grenades. It can vaporise the copper bullets before they are able to pierce the tank's casing.

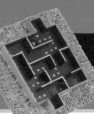

Technology Quiz

1. What network works like a giant encyclopaedia?

2. What kind of technology analyses light from the stars?

3. How is sound produced from a CD?

4. What is a tiny computer chip called?

5. From where can a guided missile be directed?

6. What are mobile phone transmitter areas called?

7. What technology is used to look at your brain?

8. Which type of animals were used to help make the first sound records?

9. What kind of machine uses light-sensitive technology?

10. What could an electro-cardiograph be used to check?

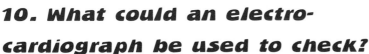

Index